# Cause, Effect and Chaos!
## In Outer Space

Author Paul Mason
with artwork by Mark Ruffle

WAYLAND
www.waylandbooks.co.uk

First published in Great Britain in 2018
by Wayland
Copyright © Hodder and Stoughton, 2018

Series editor: Paul Rockett
Series design and illustration: Mark Ruffle
www.rufflebrothers.com

HB ISBN 978 1 5263 0524 4
PB ISBN 978 1 5263 0525 1

Printed in China

Wayland, an imprint of
Hachette Children's Group
Part of Hodder and Stoughton
Carmelite House
50 Victoria Embankment
London EC4Y 0DZ

An Hachette UK Company
www.hachette.co.uk

# Contents

# Cause and Effect

What causes events to happen? Usually they are the effect of something that happened just before.

You can probably think of a few examples from your own life:

## You study hard
at school, or you train hard at gymnastics, football or ballet.

You get a good grade, or finally do a backflip, score a goal or perform a perfect pirouette.

## Of course, not every action has a good effect:

You 'borrow' your mum's iPad and 'accidentally' download a paid-for app.

No pocket money for a month.

Chaos with your social plans! No more cinema or trips to the shops.

4

Down here on Earth, cause and effect is sometimes painful – and sometimes even deadly. So just imagine what things are like in *outer space!*

The Earth is slowly moving further from the Sun.

If Earth moves too far away, we will lose the Sun's heat. Everyone will freeze to death!

Fortunately, big events in outer space happen slowly. For example, we are only moving 15 cm from the Sun each year. It will be a very long time before this is a problem.

# Solar Flare!

Most humans feel happy on a sunny day. No wonder – like every other living thing, we actually need sunshine to survive.

Sunshine is a kind of energy that comes from the Sun, the star at the centre of our solar system.

Convective zone

Photosphere The energy arrives in the Sun's photosphere, which is hotter and brighter than the biggest fire you can imagine.

Radiative zone

The energy travels out to the surface, called the photosphere. A lot of heat is lost, so the temperature there is only a roasting 10,000°C.

Core

In the Sun's core, a **chemical reaction** produces huge amounts of energy. The temperature here is about **15,000,000°C!**

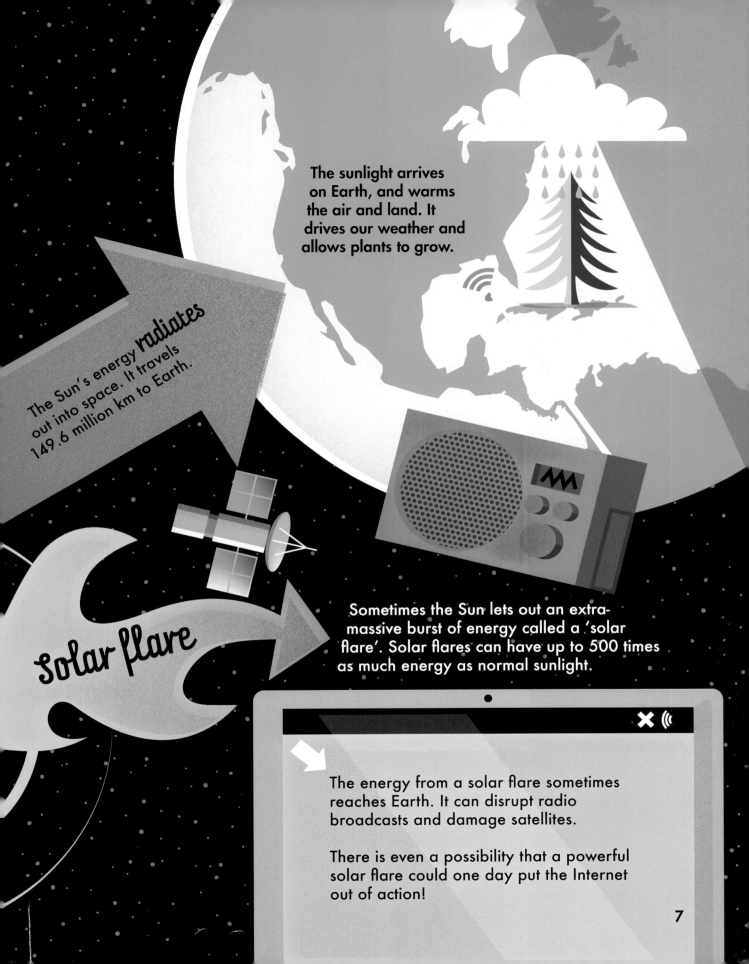

The sunlight arrives on Earth, and warms the air and land. It drives our weather and allows plants to grow.

The Sun's energy **radiates** out into space. It travels 149.6 million km to Earth.

*Solar flare*

Sometimes the Sun lets out an extra-massive burst of energy called a 'solar flare'. Solar flares can have up to 500 times as much energy as normal sunlight.

The energy from a solar flare sometimes reaches Earth. It can disrupt radio broadcasts and damage satellites.

There is even a possibility that a powerful solar flare could one day put the Internet out of action!

# When the Sun Goes Out

Without sunshine, plants would not grow and there would be no weather or seasons. Planet Earth would be just another cold, dark rock travelling through space.

Two celestial bodies move through our sky in daytime:

the **Sun and the Moon.**

The Moon moves slowly, the Sun often catches up with it.

Sometimes as the Sun catches up it goes behind the Moon. When it is partly behind, there is a strange half-light down on Earth.*

*The Sun is 400 times wider than the Moon. They appear the same size because the Sun is also 400 times further away.

If the **Sun** carries on and goes right behind the Moon, its light is blocked out completely. This is called

## a total eclipse.

A giant shadow 160 km across falls on the Earth's surface. At the heart of the shadow it is suddenly like night-time.

**A total eclipse** happens somewhere on Earth about every 18 months.

This sudden darkness tricks animals into thinking night has come.

Birds rush to their nests. Night-time insects start chirping and tweeting. Spiders start taking down their webs. There are even reports that hippos get scared and hide underwater!

# Meteorite Mayhem!

When you look up into the night-time sky, you might see what looks like a star shooting through space. It's actually a meteor heading towards the Earth!

A meteor begins life as a **meteoroid** – a piece of space rock that has come away from an asteroid or comet.

When a meteor falls into the Earth's atmosphere it becomes a meteor.

Asteroid

Meteoroid

As the meteor falls, friction between the rock and gases in Earth's atmosphere causes it to heat up and glow. This is what makes the meteor visible.

Several meteors all falling towards Earth at the same time are called a **meteor shower**.

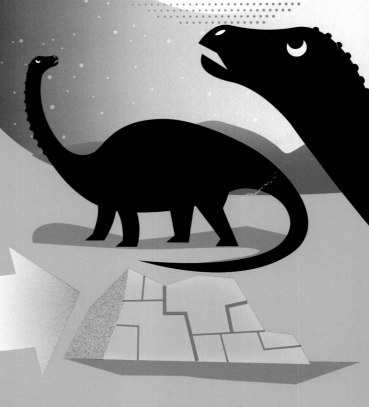

10 km

Most meteors burn up and become dust before they can hit the Earth's surface.

Space dust from meteors falls to Earth every day.

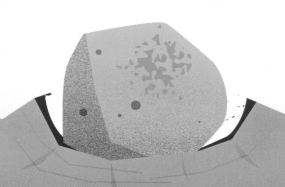

A meteor that hits the Earth is called a

*meteorite*.

Some scientists think that 65 million years ago a 10-km-wide meteorite hit the Earth, causing massive dust clouds, fires and tsunamis. They believe this caused the dinosaurs to become extinct.

# Mission to the Moon

In 1969, three astronauts went to the Moon.
Their mission was called Apollo 11.

The astronauts were Buzz Aldrin,
Neil Armstrong and Michael Collins.
No one was sure if they could reach
the Moon – or make it home again alive.

Five powerful rockets blasted the
Moon mission away from Earth.
When they ran out of fuel
the rockets were
*jettisoned*.

Five more rockets
started. Earth's
gravity was weaker
at this point, so
these rockets were
smaller. They too
were jettisoned.

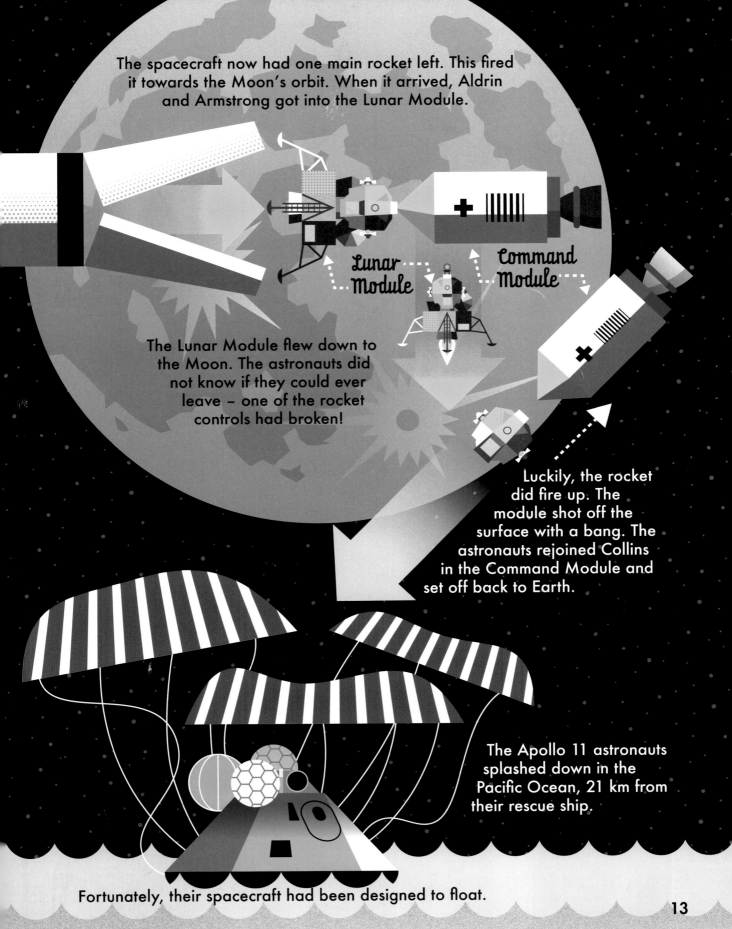

The spacecraft now had one main rocket left. This fired it towards the Moon's orbit. When it arrived, Aldrin and Armstrong got into the Lunar Module.

Lunar Module

Command Module

The Lunar Module flew down to the Moon. The astronauts did not know if they could ever leave – one of the rocket controls had broken!

Luckily, the rocket did fire up. The module shot off the surface with a bang. The astronauts rejoined Collins in the Command Module and set off back to Earth.

The Apollo 11 astronauts splashed down in the Pacific Ocean, 21 km from their rescue ship.

Fortunately, their spacecraft had been designed to float.

# Space Life

Today, scientists and astronauts no longer visit the Moon. Instead, they live in space. The record is 437 days* in space – well over a year!

Our bodies are designed for living with Earth's gravity, but in space there is no gravity. So, what effect does living in space have on a human?

On the **space station** there is no gravity to help blood flow downwards. Instead, extra blood stays in the upper body and head. The astronauts' faces quickly become puffy.

When the spacecraft blasts off, some astronauts feel nauseous as the launch vehicle climbs into Earth's atmosphere.

With **extra blood** in their upper bodies, there is less in the astronauts' legs. Their legs shrink, becoming wrinkled and thin.

*Set by Valeri Polyakov, from January 1994 to March 1995.

14

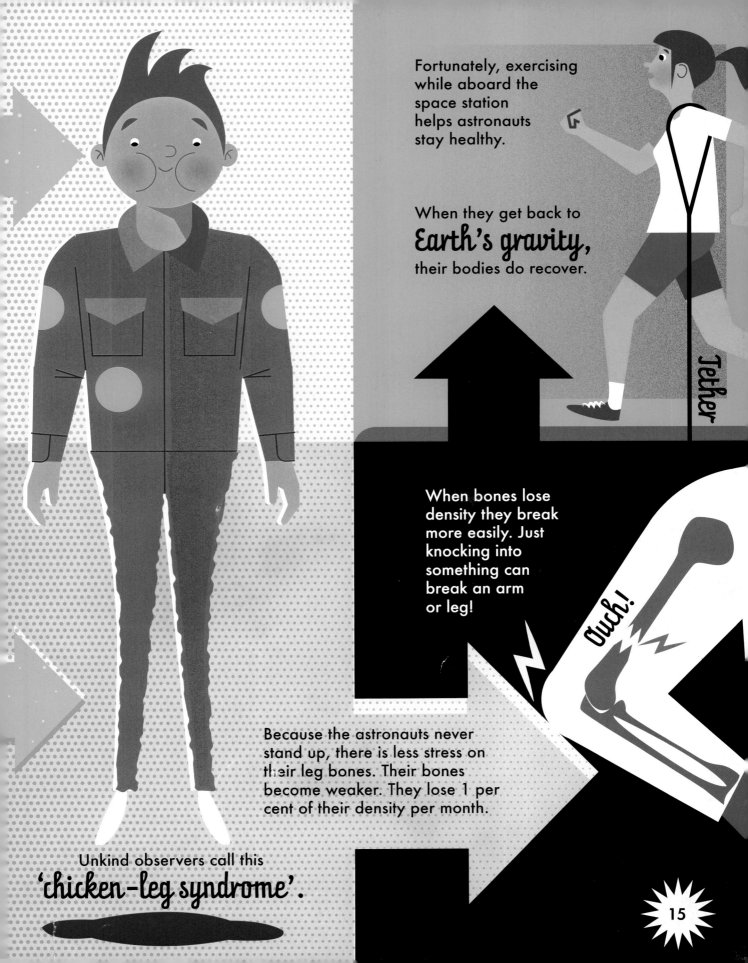

Fortunately, exercising while aboard the space station helps astronauts stay healthy.

When they get back to **Earth's gravity,** their bodies do recover.

Tether

When bones lose density they break more easily. Just knocking into something can break an arm or leg!

Ouch!

Because the astronauts never stand up, there is less stress on their leg bones. Their bones become weaker. They lose 1 per cent of their density per month.

Unkind observers call this **'chicken-leg syndrome'.**

15

# Having a Wee in Zero-G

Aboard a space station, gravity does not pull you downwards as it does on Earth. You actually feel zero gravity – often called zero-G.

With zero-G, everything that isn't fixed in place just floats off! Even simple activities become complicated. Activities like putting ketchup on food, spitting out toothpaste, washing … and having …

… a wee.

First, the astronaut switches on a fan at the end of a long, flexible pipe. The fan sucks air into the pipe.

Now the astronaut has a wee – with the pipe VERY close by. Otherwise the wee just floats off!

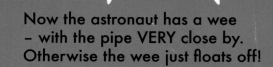

**Steam**

**Steam**

Contaminants

Contaminants

Once enough has been collected, the wee is heated to boiling point and turns to steam.

Aboard the International Space Station, American astronauts don't just collect wee from their own side of the station. They also collect wee from the Russian side. The Russians don't want their wee, so they let the Americans have it.

The wee-steam container spins around at high speed. Any contaminants are pressed against the side of the container. The pure steam stays in the middle.

**Wee**

Wee is sucked into the space station's Urine Processing Assembly, or UPA. It is about 95 per cent water. The astronauts need the water, which is a valuable resource, back!

The steam is cooled down and turns back into liquid.

If the process has worked, the wee becomes clean water for thirsty astronauts to drink. If it hasn't, they get a nasty surprise!

$H_2O$

17

# Lost in Space!

Sometimes astronauts go outside a space station. Space boffins call this an 'extra vehicular activity' or EVA. Most people call it a space walk.

A space walk begins when the astronaut goes outside through an air lock.

The inner door is closed, to keep air inside the space station. Then the outer door is opened and the astronaut climbs out.

The astronaut clips on a 'safety tether', a line attaching her or him to the space station.

If the astronaut accidentally pushes away from the space station, the tether means they are still attached to the space station.

If the tether breaks, the astronaut sails off into space.

Help!

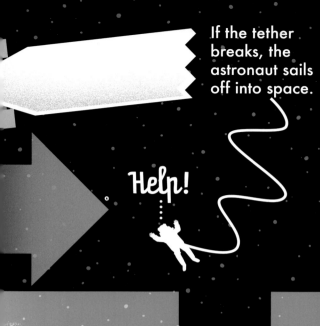

She or he will either:

**a)** run out of oxygen and water, resulting in death, or;

**b)** be sucked into Earth's gravity and burn up like a meteor, resulting in death.

So, the astronaut turns on the *jet pack* on the space suit!

Once the jet pack is on, the astronaut uses a hand-held controller – like a video-game joystick – to rocket back to safety.

The jet packs only have a small amount of fuel – but it is enough to get back to the space station or rescue someone else who has come untethered.

# Mars: Planet of War!

Mars is sometimes called the 'Red Planet' because from Earth it looks red. For centuries people have associated the colour of Mars with war.

Does Mars' red colour carry a message of war, though – or is it red for another, less worrying reason?

Iron oxide

The solar system – including Mars – formed billions of years ago. Among its chemical elements was one called *iron*.

As Mars formed, some iron was pulled into the planet's core by gravity.

The planet's weak gravity left a lot of iron at the surface. The iron at Mars' surface began to turn into iron oxide, or rust.

Core

The iron oxide was blown into the atmosphere by massive volcanic eruptions. It finally settled across practically the whole planet.

Mars' biggest volcano, **Olympus Mons,** is 21 km high.

When light hits the layer of iron oxide, blue and green colours are absorbed. Red, though, is reflected back. This is why when you look at Mars, it seems red.

Red

Blue

Green

Warlike aliens

If Mars' red colour is a signal from warlike aliens hoping to invade Earth, we need to be worried. In space terms, Mars isn't very far away!

Fortunately, there are no aliens on Mars. In fact, probes sent from Earth have found there is no life at all.

# Risky Ride to Neptune

Neptune is the planet furthest from the Sun. It's a really long way away – at least 4.3 billion km.

Using a current spacecraft, it would take about ten-and-a-half years to get to Neptune. Fortunately, there would be plenty to look at on the way, but the journey also contains many potential dangers.

**Two moons**

**Mars**

**Asteroid Belt**

The first planet you pass is Mars. Hopefully you won't end up like Mars' two moons. They were once asteroids, but got caught in Mars's gravity and couldn't leave!

As your spacecraft passes through the Asteroid Belt, be careful not to crash. Even a small collision would spell catastrophe.

Jupiter is two-and-a-half times the size of all the other planets put together. Steer well clear – Jupiter's gravity is strong! You wouldn't want to be pulled into the Great Red Spot: a violent storm so huge that three Earths could fit inside it.

# Jupiter

## The Great Red Spot

Like Jupiter, Saturn is a gas giant. Its most amazing feature is its rings, which are made mostly of ice. A giant chunk of ice could do some serious damage to your spacecraft!

Uranus is a freezing ice giant. It looks blue because of the stinky methane gas in its atmosphere. Below the methane, violent storms constantly rage.

# Uranus

# Neptune

Once you reach Neptune, you might want to come straight home again! Neptune is not exactly a tourist destination: it's freezing cold (about −200°C) and constantly whipped by winds of over 2,000 kph. No visitor could survive down there.

# Saturn

Ice

# Death of a Star

Stars get their energy from hydrogen in their core. Eventually, that hydrogen is used up.

Bigger, brighter stars use up their hydrogen more quickly than smaller ones. But whatever its size, a star's hydrogen always runs out in the end.

## Red giant

As the **hydrogen** runs out, the star swells up and glows more brightly. It becomes a red giant.

When the Sun eventually becomes a red giant (in about 5 billion years), Earth will be toast!

The star's fuel finally runs out.

## White dwarf

With ordinary stars, a layer of gas explodes outwards and the core cools down. It becomes a white dwarf.

24

When a giant star's fuel runs out, it collapses inwards. The star's matter bounces off its core, producing a massive ...

# supernova explosion!

Supernovas produce more light than a whole galaxy of normal stars – but only for about a month.

After, only the core of the supernova is left. It has such strong gravity that even light cannot escape. It becomes a 'black hole'.

Black holes have an imaginary line around them called the 'event horizon'. Once something passes the event horizon, it is impossible to escape the black hole's gravity.

Event horizon

Black hole

# Great Balls of Fire!

At the heart of our galaxy is a massive black hole. Once in a while, it spits out a star. The star, a giant, flaming ball of gas, crashes through the universe.

## But what causes this to happen?

### The black hole

has very strong gravity and is constantly pulling in space matter.

Sometimes the black hole pulls in two stars that are in orbit around each other. They are like dancers holding hands, spinning around.

As the stars are sucked towards the black hole, its gravity adds to the speed of their spinning.

Eventually the stars spin so fast that they cannot stay together. It's as if the dancers have suddenly let go.

One star is sucked into the black hole. The other is flung away at high speed.

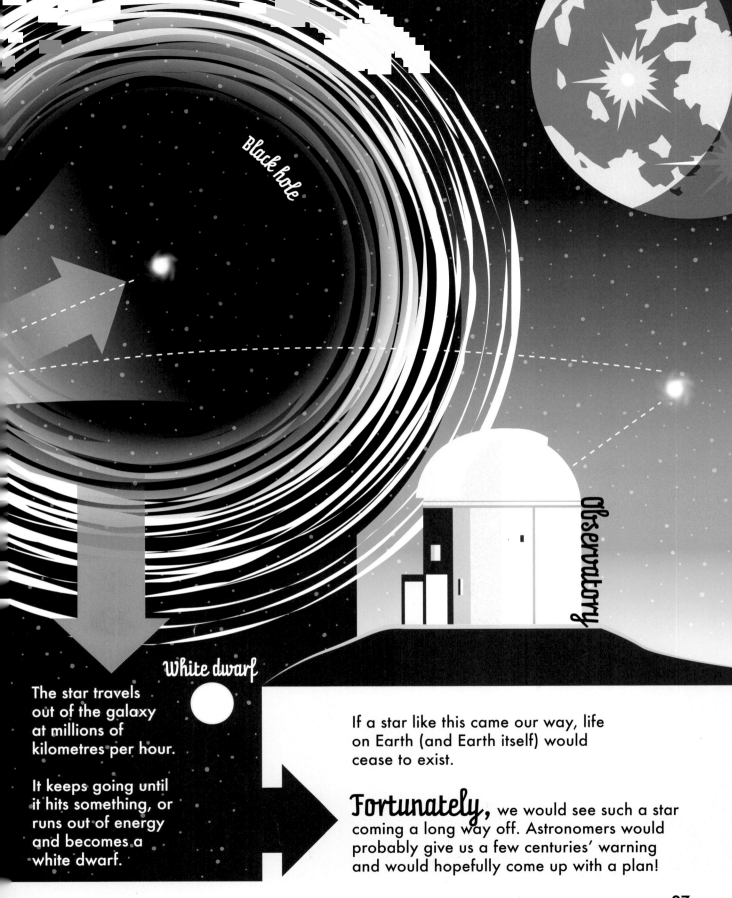

Black hole

Observatory

White dwarf

The star travels out of the galaxy at millions of kilometres per hour.

It keeps going until it hits something, or runs out of energy and becomes a white dwarf.

If a star like this came our way, life on Earth (and Earth itself) would cease to exist.

**Fortunately,** we would see such a star coming a long way off. Astronomers would probably give us a few centuries' warning and would hopefully come up with a plan!

# The Galactic Cannibals

Did you know that galaxies can 'eat' each other?
This process has the brilliant name 'galactic cannibalism'.

Galactic cannibalism starts when a small galaxy is close
to a much bigger galaxy.

Big galaxies have very strong gravity. This gravity pulls on smaller galaxies nearby.

The smaller galaxy is slowly drawn towards the cannibal.

When the small galaxy gets close enough, its own gravity can no longer hold its
stars and planets in place. They start to be attracted by the cannibal galaxy instead.

The small galaxy slowly breaks up and becomes part of the bigger galaxy.

It takes billions of years for one galaxy to eat another.

Unfortunately, our galaxy, the Milky Way, has a **MUCH** bigger next-door neighbour: Andromeda.

Andromeda has already smashed into and eaten at least one other galaxy, maybe more. And Andromeda is heading our way at 300 km per second.

Andromeda

Milky Way

When Andromeda arrives it will cause galactic chaos. The whole Milky Way will be wrecked!

**Fortunately,** Andromeda won't be arriving for about a billion years.

# Glossary

**air lock** small space with doors at opposite sides, so one door can be shut and sealed before the other is opened

**astronomer** person who studies the planets, stars and other celestial bodies

**celestial body** any natural space object that can be seen by astronomers

**chemical element** basic chemical unit which cannot be broken down into something else

**chemical reaction** process of substances changing into something else, such as metal rusting or wood burning

**contaminant** polluting or poisonous substance

**density** describes how tightly packed the inside of an object is. A car with five people in it has greater density than a car with only two people, for example

**gas giant** large planet made mainly of gas

**gravity** force of attraction of an object; gravity depends on an object's size, with greater size producing more gravity

**ice giant** large planet made mainly of frozen matter

**jettison** cast off or away

**Lunar Module** landing craft for visiting the Moon's surface

**meteor** meteoroid (a piece of space rock) that falls into the Earth's atmosphere

**meteorite** meteor that hits Earth's surface

**Moon orbit** curved path around the Moon

**nauseous** feeling sick, as though wanting to vomit

**orbit** circular path around another object, where the object's gravity and your own speed are in balance

**radiate** spread outwards

**red giant** star that has swelled and glows red after its supply of hydrogen has run out

**resource** useable supply of something, such as water, air or food

**syndrome** group of medical symptoms

**tether** cord or strap used to hold an object in place. In gravity-free space, tethers come in very handy

**white dwarf** small, very dense star

**zero-G** short for 'zero gravity'

# Finding Out More

## Space places

**The National Space Centre**
Exploration Drive
Leicester LE4 5NS

This is a fantastic place if you're into space. It has great exhibits, from the 'Space Oddities' section where you can see all sorts of unusual space gear and use a touch table to explore, to the Rocket Tower with its real space rockets and an Apollo Lunar Module.

The Space Centre also has a website at **spacecentre.co.uk**

**The Science Museum**
Exhibition Road
South Kensington
London SW7 2DD

The Science Museum's 'Exploring Space' section has rockets, satellites and even a replica of *Eagle*, the Lunar Module that took Aldrin and Armstrong to the Moon. You can also find out about the nitty-gritty of living in space: having a wash, cooking, going to the toilet.

The Science Museum's website is at **sciencemuseum.org.uk**

## Space books

*100 Things To Know About Space*, Alex Frith, Jerome Martin and Alice James (Usborne, 2016)
Great, colourful illustrations and infographics, plus a lot of facts about space that might surprise you, make this a great way to find out all sorts of facts a budding astronomer will find fascinating.

*How To Bluff Your Way Into Space*, Paul Mason (Oxford University Press, 2014)
A guide to fitting in with the other astronauts even if you haven't exactly done the same years and years of training as them. From not giving yourself away by calling your launch vehicle a 'rocket ship' to the correct etiquette for going to the loo (always change the plastic bag!), this book is full of useful advice.

*How To Design The World's Best Space Station In 10 Simple Steps*, Paul Mason (Wayland, 2016)
Imagine you get left a gazillion pounds and decide to build yourself a space station. Not just any space station: the world's best. Where do you start? With this book, is where!

The *Watch This Space* series by Clive Gifford (Wayland, 2016) contains four fun-and-fact-filled books on *The Solar System, Meteors and Comets; Stars, Galaxies and the Milky Way; The Universe, Black Holes and the Big Bang;* and *Astronomy, Astronauts and Space Exploration.*

# Index

# Cause, Effect and Chaos!

## Titles in this series:

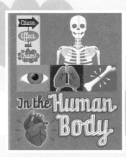